Introducción a los padres

We Both Read es la primera serie de libros diseñada para invitar a padres e hijos a compartir la lectura de un cuento, por turnos y en voz alta. Esta "lectura compartida" —que se ha desarrollado en conjunto con especialistas en primeras lecturas— invita a los padres a leer los textos más complejos en la página de la izquierda; luego, les toca a los niños leer las páginas de la derecha, que contienen textos más sencillos, escritos específicamente para primeros lectores.

Leer en voz alta es una de las actividades más importantes que los padres comparten con sus hijos para ayudarlos a desarrollar la lectura. Sin embargo, *We Both Read* no es solo leerle *a* un niño, sino que les permite a los padres leer *con* el niño. *We Both Read* es más poderoso y efectivo porque combina dos elementos claves del aprendizaje: "demostración" (el padre lee) y "aplicación" (el niño lee). El resultado no es solo que el niño aprende a leer más rápido, ¡sino que ambos disfrutan y se enriquecen con esta experiencia!

Sería más útil si usted lee el libro completo y en voz alta la primera vez, y luego invita a su niño a participar en una segunda lectura. En algunos libros, las palabras más difíciles se presentan por primera vez en **negritas** en el texto del padre. Señalar o hablar sobre estas palabras ayudará a su niño a familiarizarse con ellas y a ampliar su vocabulario. También notará que el ícono "lee el padre" ⊙ precede el texto del padre y el ícono "lee el niño" ◔ precede el texto del niño.

Lo animamos a compartir e interactuar con su niño mientras leen el libro juntos. Si su hijo tiene dificultad, usted puede mencionar algunas cosas que lo ayuden. "Decir cada sonido" es bueno, pero puede que esto no funcione con todas las palabras. Los niños pueden hallar pistas en las palabras del cuento, en el contexto de las oraciones e incluso en las imágenes. Algunos cuentos incluyen patrones y rimas que los ayudarán. También le podría ser útil a su niño tocar las palabras con su dedo mientras lee, para conectar mejor el sonido de la voz con la palabra impresa.

¡Al compartir los libros de *We Both Read*, usted y su hijo vivirán juntos la fascinante aventura de la lectura! Es una manera divertida y fácil de animar y ayudar a su niño a leer —¡y una maravillosa manera de preparar a su niño para disfrutar de la lectura durante toda su vida!

Parent's Introduction

We Both Read is the first series of books designed to invite parents and children to share the reading of a story by taking turns reading aloud. This "shared reading" innovation, which was developed with reading education specialists, invites parents to read the more complex text and story line on the left-hand pages. Then, children can be encouraged to read the right-hand pages, which feature text written for a specific early reading level.

Reading aloud is one of the most important activities parents can share with their child to assist them in their reading development. However, *We Both Read* goes beyond reading *to* a child and allows parents to share the reading *with* a child. *We Both Read* is so powerful and effective because it combines two key elements in learning: "modeling" (the parent reads) and "doing" (the child reads). The result is not only faster reading development for the child, but a much more enjoyable and enriching experience for both!

You may find it helpful to read the entire book aloud yourself the first time, then invite your child to participate in the second reading. In some books, a few more difficult words will first be introduced in the parent's text, distinguished with bold lettering. Pointing out, and even discussing, these words will help familiarize your child with them and help to build your child's vocabulary. Also, note that a "talking parent" icon ⓒ precedes the parent's text, and a "talking child" icon ⓒ precedes the child's text.

We encourage you to share and interact with your child as you read the book together. If your child is having difficulty, you might want to mention a few things to help him. "Sounding out" is good, but it will not work with all words. Children can pick up clues about the words they are reading from the story, the context of the sentence, or even the pictures. Some stories have rhyming patterns that might help. It might also help them to touch the words with their finger as they read, to better connect the voice sound and the printed word.

Sharing the *We Both Read* books together will engage you and your child in an interactive adventure in reading! It is a fun and easy way to encourage and help your child to read—and a wonderful way to start them off on a lifetime of reading enjoyment!

Baseball Fever
La fiebre del béisbol

A We Both Read® Book
Bilingual in English and Spanish

We Both Read® is a trademark of Treasure Bay, Inc.
Editorial Services by Cambridge BrickHouse, Inc.
Bilingual adaptation © 2018 by Treasure Bay, Inc.

Published by
Treasure Bay, Inc.
P.O. Box 119
Novato, CA 94948 USA

Printed in Malaysia

Library of Congress Catalog Card Number: 2017947067

ISBN: 978-1-60115-090-5

Visit us online at:
www.TreasureBayBooks.com

PR-10-17

WE BOTH READ®

Baseball Fever
La fiebre del béisbol

By Sindy McKay

Illustrated by Meredith Johnson

Translated by Manuel Alemán

TREASURE BAY

The clock in my classroom moved slowly toward three o'clock. It **always** moved slowly on baseball practice days.

BBRRRIIIING! The bell finally rang. I grabbed my backpack and raced toward the field as fast as I could!

*El reloj de mi salón se acercaba lentamente a las tres. **Siempre** se movía con lentitud los días de práctica de béisbol.*

¡RIIIIIIIING! Por fin sonó el timbre. ¡Agarré mi mochila y corrí al campo de juego tan rápido como pude!

   I was going to be the first one there. I was almost **always** the first one there, but not today.

*Iba a ser el primero en llegar. Yo casi **siempre** era el primero, pero no esta vez.*

Karen Washington, the best shortstop around, got there before me. She waved and yelled, "Hi Jason!"

I answered her with a great big sneeze!

"Whoa, are you okay?" she asked.

I told her I was fine. Then I ran to the **pitcher's** mound to get in some practice before **Coach** Bill arrived.

Karen Washington, el mejor campo corto de la zona, llegó antes que yo. Ella saludó y gritó: —¡Hola, Jason!

¡Le respondí con un gran estornudo!

—Caramba, ¿estás bien? —preguntó.

*Le dije que estaba bien. Luego corrí al montículo del **lanzador** para calentar un poco antes de que el **entrenador** Bill llegara.*

Coach Bill was a great coach. He made our team a great team. He made me a great **pitcher**!

*El **entrenador** Bill era un gran entrenador. Hizo de nuestro equipo un gran equipo. ¡A mí me hizo un gran **lanzador**!*

5

Coach Bill sent four of us to the outfield while the rest of the team lined up for batting practice. Karen stepped up and hit a high fly, right to me.

"I've got it!" I called as I moved under the ball. Then I **sneezed**.

El entrenador Bill envió a cuatro de nosotros al campo mientras el resto del equipo formó una fila para la práctica de bateo. Karen se acercó y bateó una bola alta directo hacia mí.

—¡La tengo! —grité mientras me movía bajo la bola. Luego **estornudé**.

I **sneezed** hard. Then I sneezed again—and again.

The ball hit the dirt at my feet.

Estornudé fuerte. Luego volví a estornudar una, y otra vez.

La pelota golpeó el suelo a mis pies.

Coach Bill ran out to see if I was okay.

"Looks like you're getting sick, Jason," he said. "You better go home and take care of yourself. Saturday is our first game of the season, and I don't want you to miss it!"

El entrenador Bill corrió a ver si yo estaba bien.

—Parece que te vas a enfermar, Jason —dijo—. Será mejor que vayas a casa y te cuides. El sábado es nuestro primer juego de la temporada, ¡y no quiero que te lo pierdas!

I didn't want to go home, but Coach Bill said I had to.

I didn't want to be sick, but I was.

Yo no quería irme a casa, pero el entrenador Bill dijo que tenía que hacerlo.

Yo no quería estar enfermo, pero lo estaba.

That night at dinner, Mom noticed I wasn't eating my peas. I love peas — but they tasted kind of yucky tonight. Mom frowned and reached across the table to feel my forehead. "Do you feel okay?" she asked.

Esa noche, durante la cena, mamá notó que no me estaba comiendo mis guisantes. —Me encantan los guisantes, pero esa noche no me sabían bien. Mamá frunció el ceño y extendió su mano para tocar mi frente. —¿Te sientes bien? —preguntó.

"I feel fine," I said. "I feel great!" Then I sneezed again.

Mom sent me right to bed.

—Me siento bien —dije—. ¡Me siento muy bien! Luego volví a estornudar.

Mamá me envió directamente a la cama.

11

When I woke up the next morning I didn't feel so good. My throat was scratchy and my nose was stuffy, and I didn't really feel like going to school or to **baseball practice** or anything. I just wanted to crawl under my covers and go back to sleep.

*Cuando me desperté, a la mañana siguiente, no me sentía nada bien. Tenía picazón en la garganta y la nariz tupida, y no me sentía como para ir a la escuela ni a la **práctica del béisbol**, ni a nada. Solo quería acurrucarme bajo las mantas y volver a dormir.*

Mom came in my room. I told her I felt great! "I can't wait to go to school," I said. "I can't wait to go to **baseball practice**."

Mamá entró en mi habitación. ¡Le dije que me sentía muy bien!

*—Estoy ansioso por ir a la escuela —dije—. Estoy ansioso por ir a la **práctica de béisbol**.*

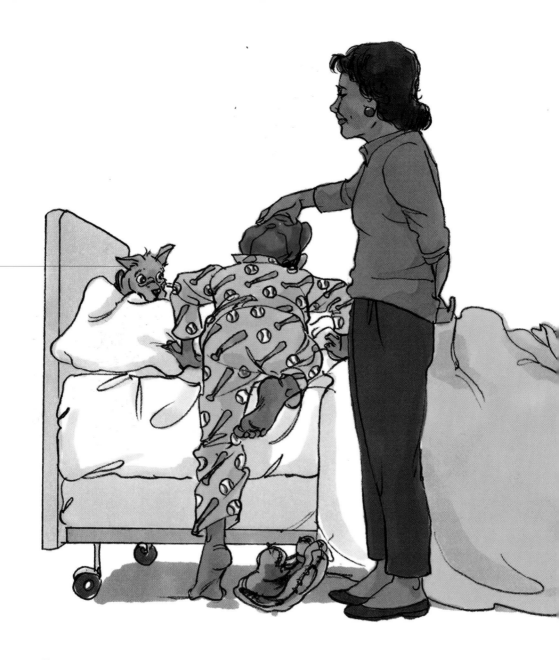

Mom said I looked miserable. She informed me there would be no school this morning and there would definitely be no baseball practice this afternoon.

Mamá dijo que yo me veía muy mal. Ella me informó que no habría escuela esa mañana y, definitivamente, no habría práctica de béisbol esa tarde.

You just can't fool my mom.

Mi madre no es fácil de engañar.

Mom tucked me back under the covers and took my temperature.

"You have a little **fever**," she said. "I'll get you some medicine. You try to get some rest."

Mamá me metió debajo de las sábanas y me puso el termómetro.

*—Tienes un poco de **fiebre** —dijo—. Te daré una medicina. Intenta descansar un poco.*

I didn't want to have a **fever**. So I got some rest. When I woke up, I told Mom I felt great! But she still didn't let me go to baseball practice.

*No quería tener **fiebre**. Así que descansé un poco. Cuando me desperté, le dije a mamá que ¡me sentía muy bien! Pero ella no me dejó ir a la práctica de béisbol.*

17

That evening Karen Washington called.

"We missed you today," she said. "Tim Anderson is working on his **fastball,** but he hasn't quite mastered the grip yet. I hope you feel better in time for the game on Saturday."

Esa noche Karen Washington llamó.
*—Te extrañamos hoy —dijo—. Tim Anderson está trabajando en su **bola rápida**, pero todavía no tiene control sobre ella. Espero que te sientas mejor para el partido del sábado.*

It felt good to know they missed me. It felt good to know they missed my **fastball**.

I just had to get well in time for the game!

*Me daba gusto saber que me extrañaron. Me daba gusto saber que extrañaron mi **bola rápida**.*

¡Solo tenía que recuperarme pronto para el juego!

19

I tried to go to sleep early that night. But every time I laid my head down, I started to cough. Mom said if I didn't feel better in the **morning**, she'd take me to see the **doctor**. I finally fell asleep and had a great dream about pitching a no-hitter in front of a big crowd!

*Traté de dormirme temprano esa noche. Pero cada vez que recostaba la cabeza, empezaba a toser. Mamá dijo que si no me sentía mejor por la **mañana**, me llevaría al **doctor**. Finalmente me quedé dormido y tuve un gran sueño: ¡lanzaba un juego perfecto frente a una gran multitud!*

The next **morning** I felt great! Then I got out of bed. I didn't feel so great anymore.

Mom took me to see the **doctor**.

¡A la **mañana** siguiente me sentía genial! Entonces me levanté de la cama. Pero no me sentía tan genial.

Mamá me llevó al **doctor**.

We arrived at Dr. Elman's office and waited until the nurse came out and called my name. She took us back into an examination room and asked me some questions, then took my **temperature** with a really cool-looking thermometer.

*Llegamos a la oficina del Dr. Elman y esperamos hasta que la enfermera me llamó. Nos llevó a una sala de reconocimiento y me hizo algunas preguntas, luego tomó mi **temperatura** con un termómetro muy gracioso.*

She put it in my ear and waited until it went "beep." Then she took it out and smiled.

"Your **temperature** is good," she said.

Ella me lo puso en el oído y esperó hasta que sonó un pitido. Luego lo sacó y sonrió.

*—Tu **temperatura** está bien —dijo.*

She told us Dr. Elman would be in to see us in just a few minutes, then left.

While we waited, I explored the exam room. There were lots of cabinets and a sink with a funny faucet you could turn on by pressing pedals with your feet. And there were **posters** on the walls.

Ella nos dijo que el Dr. Elman vendría a vernos en unos minutos, y se fue.

*Mientras esperábamos, exploré la sala de reconocimiento. Había un montón de gabinetes y un fregadero con un grifo muy gracioso que podía abrirse pisando un pedal. Y había **carteles** en las paredes.*

One **poster** was about food. Another poster showed where the food goes in your body. The biggest poster was the best one I had ever seen!

*Un **cartel** trataba sobre los alimentos. Otro mostraba adónde van los alimentos en tu cuerpo. ¡El cartel más grande era el mejor que había visto en mi vida!*

"That's Cy Young, the greatest pitcher that ever lived."

I turned around to find **Dr. Elman** standing in the doorway, grinning.

"I just got that poster last week," he continued. "You like it?"

—Ese es Cy Young, el mejor lanzador de todos los tiempos.
*Me volví y vi al **Dr. Elman** parado en la puerta, sonriendo.*
—Acabo de recibir ese cartel la semana pasada —continuó—.
¿Te gusta?

"Like it?" I said. "I LOVE it! I'm a pitcher too, you know."

Dr. Elman smiled. "Yes, I know."

—¿*Que si me gusta?* —*dije*— *¡ME ENCANTA! Yo también soy lanzador, ¿sabe?*

El **Dr. Elman** *sonrió.* —*Sí, lo sé.*

I smiled back and told him that was why he had to make me better today. "I just have to pitch in the first game of the season tomorrow!"

Dr. Elman said he couldn't make any promises, but he would do his best. Then he started the examination.

Le sonreí y le dije que por eso él tenía que curarme ese día.

—¡Yo tengo que lanzar en el primer juego de la temporada, mañana!

El Dr. Elman dijo que no podía prometerme nada, pero que haría todo lo posible. Luego comenzó a examinarme.

He looked in my ears. He looked in my eyes. He looked at my throat. He felt my neck. He even looked up my nose!

Examinó mis oídos. Examinó mis ojos. Examinó mi garganta. Me palpó el cuello. ¡Y hasta examinó mi nariz!

Then he listened to my heart and told me to take deep breaths while he listened to my lungs.

"What do you hear?" I asked anxiously. "Will I be okay by **tomorrow**?"

"Hmmm . . . I think I hear the roar of the crowd at a baseball game," he answered with a grin.

Luego auscultó mi corazón y me dijo que respirara profundo mientras auscultaba mis pulmones.

*—¿Qué oye? —le pregunté ansioso—. ¿Estaré bien **mañana**?*

—Mmmm. . . Creo que escucho el rugido de la multitud en un partido de béisbol —respondió con una sonrisa.

"Does that mean I can play **tomorrow**?"

Dr. Elman shook his head. "I'm sorry, Jason," he said. "You will be fine, but not by tomorrow."

—¿*Eso significa que puedo jugar **mañana**?*

El Dr. Elman movió la cabeza. —*Lo siento, Jason* —*dijo*—. *Estarás bien, pero no mañana.*

31

He told my mother that it didn't look like anything serious, but I should stay in bed over the weekend. Then he turned to me and said, "I wish I knew of some way to get you better in time for the game tomorrow, but I'm afraid there's still no cure for the common cold."

Le dijo a mi madre que no parecía nada serio, pero que debía permanecer en cama durante el fin de semana. Luego se volvió hacia mí y me dijo: —Me gustaría saber cómo curarte a tiempo para el juego de mañana, pero me temo que todavía no hay cura para el resfriado común.

He did wish he could help me. I could tell.

"It's okay, Dr. Elman," I told him. "It's just a game."

Then Mom and I went home.

Él quería ayudarme. Yo podría asegurarlo.

—Está bien, Dr. Elman —le dije—. Es solo un juego.

Luego mamá y yo nos fuimos a casa.

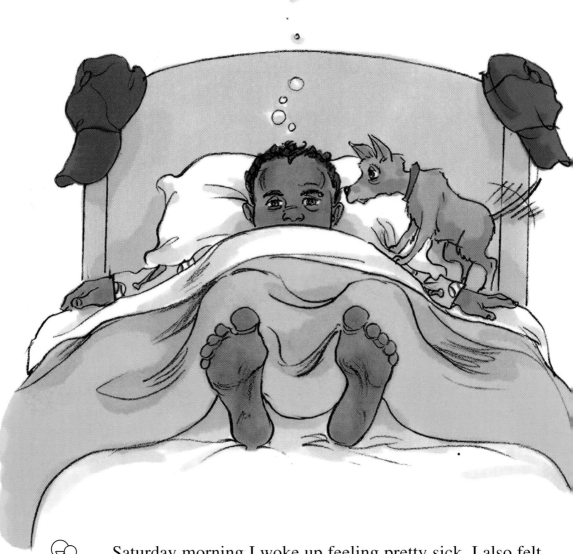

Saturday morning I woke up feeling pretty sick. I also felt really sad about missing the first game of the season. Then I heard the **phone** ring. After a moment, I heard my mom's **voice** calling up to me.

*El sábado por la mañana me desperté sintiéndome muy enfermo. También me sentía muy triste por haber perdido el primer partido de la temporada. Entonces sonó el **teléfono**. Después, escuché la **voz** de mi madre llamándome.*

"It's for you, Jason," Mom said.

She gave me the **phone**, and I said, "Hello?"

"Hi, Jason," said a **voice**. "It's Karen!"

—Es para ti, Jason —dijo mamá.

Me dio el **teléfono** y dije: —¿Hola?

—Hola, Jason —dijo una **voz**—. ¡Es Karen!

Karen Washington was calling me from the baseball field!

"We're still in the first **inning** of the game," she reported. "Tim Anderson is pitching and he's doing great! We tagged a runner out on first and Dan caught a fly ball and Tim actually struck somebody out!"

¡Karen Washington me estaba llamando desde el terreno de béisbol!

*—Todavía estamos en la primera **entrada** —me dijo—. Tim Anderson está lanzando ¡y lo está haciendo muy bien! Sacamos a un corredor en primera, Dan capturó un fly elevado ¡y Tim ponchó a uno de ellos!*

"I have to go now," she said. "Coach Bill says I'm up next! I'll call you back next **inning**."

—*Tengo que dejarte ahora —dijo—. ¡El entrenador Bill dice que es mi turno al bate! Te llamaré en la próxima **entrada**.*

It was fantastic! Every inning someone on the team called me to fill me in on what was happening. It wasn't quite as good as being there in person, but it was **really** close. Even my mom wanted to hear the next report!

*¡Era fantástico! Cada entrada alguien del equipo me llamaba para actualizarme en lo que estaba ocurriendo. No era lo mismo que estar en el juego, pero era **realmente** casi igual. ¡Incluso mi mamá quería escuchar el próximo reporte!*

Our team played **really** well. The other team also played well, but we must have played better because... we won the game!

*Nuestro equipo jugó **realmente** muy bien. El otro equipo también jugó bien, pero seguro que nosotros jugamos mejor porque... ¡ganamos el juego!*

Mom said she was really sorry I couldn't be there to
celebrate with my friends.

"It's okay," I said. "There will be lots of other games."

*Mamá dijo que realmente lamentaba que yo no pudiera
estar allí para celebrar con mis amigos.*

—Está bien —le dije—. Habrá muchos otros juegos.

Playing ball is really fun. So is winning. But the very best part of baseball is having such good, good friends.

Jugar a la pelota es muy divertido. También lo es ganar. Pero lo mejor del béisbol es tener tan buenos, pero tan buenos amigos.

41

If you liked **Baseball Fever,** here are some other
We Both Read® books you are sure to enjoy!

*Si te gustó **La fiebre del béisbol,** hay aquí otros
libros de la serie We Both Read ¡que seguro vas a disfrutar!*

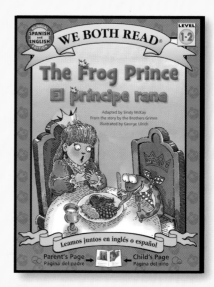

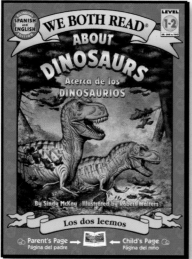

To see all the We Both Read books that are available,
just go online to **www.WeBothRead.com**.

*Para ver todos los libros disponibles de la serie
We Both Read, visite* www.webothread.com.

GREAT TALES FROM LONG AGO

ODYSSEUS AND THE ENCHANTERS

Retold by Catherine Storr
Illustrated by Mike Codd

Methuen Children's Books
in association with Belitha Press Ltd.

FAR AWAY IN THE SEAS AROUND GREECE,
lay a small island covered with thick forests.
Men told strange tales about it.
"Sailors who land there are never seen again,"
said one old man.
"Nonsense! My son was there once
and he saw lions and wolves roaming the woods.
They looked wild, but when they saw my son
they stood on their hind legs like men,"
said another man.

O DYSSEUS, THE CLEVEREST OF THE GREEK HEROES,
was sailing back after the Trojan war
to rocky Ithaca, his kingdom.
When he reached the mysterious island,
he was exhausted, after escaping great dangers.

FOR TWO DAYS, HE LAY ON THE BEACH,
getting back his strength.
On the third day,
Odysseus took his spear and his sword
and climbed the cliffs to see what the island was like.

He reached the top of a hill
from which he could see the whole island.
From among the thickly planted trees,
he saw a wisp of smoke rising into the clear air.
He went back to the shore,
carrying meat for his hungry companions,
and that night they ate and drank and were refreshed.

THE NEXT MORNING,
Odysseus divided the ship's company
into two parties of twenty-two men in each.
They cast lots, and it fell to Eurylochus,
one of the officers, to take his party of men
to explore the island.
Odysseus and the others stayed on the shore.

Eurylochus and his men climbed the hill
and they, too, saw the smoke
rising from among the trees.
As they approached, they saw a beautiful palace
in a clearing of the forest.
From the open windows of the palace
came the sound of someone singing a sweet song.
They were astonished to see the palace surrounded
by mountain wolves and lions,
who came towards them, wagging their tails
and trying to caress them.
The sailors ran for safety towards the palace.
The doors opened, and a beautiful woman
stood there and invited them to come in.

Almost all the men followed her into the palace.
Eurylochus was the only one who stayed outside,
fearing that this might be a trap.
He looked through a window, and saw Circe, the witch-goddess,
give the men a sweet drink, mixed with a drug
which made them forget their country, their wives, their children.
Then she touched them with her wand,
and drove them to the pigsties.
For each one had become a pig,
with pigs' bristles and a pig's snout.
They could not speak, they could only grunt.

Eurylochus was horrified.
He rushed back to the shore to tell Odysseus.
Odysseus took his sword and his bow
and set off alone towards Circe's palace.

As HE WENT, HE SAW A BEAUTIFUL YOUNG MAN IN HIS PATH.
The young man took his hand, and said,
"Odysseus, do not look for your companions here.
Circe, the witch-goddess,
has penned them into her sties, like swine.
She will do the same for you
if you do not do exactly what I tell you.
I am going to give you something
that will keep you safe from Circe's magic.
When she tries to turn you, too, into a pig,
draw your sword and threaten to kill her.
Make her promise to release your companions
and not to try any more of her tricks."
The young man bent down and picked a little plant.
Its petals were milk-white and its root was black.
He said, "This herb is called Moly,
and it will protect you.
It is difficult for men to dig up,
but we gods can do anything."
Then Odysseus knew that this was no ordinary man,
but Hermes, the messenger of the gods.

As ODYSSEUS APPROACHED CIRCE'S PALACE
he heard the witch-goddess, singing at her loom.
He called out, and Circe came to the door
and welcomed him, as she had his companions.
She led him in, and gave him a rich drink
in a golden bowl.
Then she touched him with her wand, and said,
"Go and join your friends in the sty."
But the herb, Moly, protected Odysseus,
and he remained in his own shape, as a man.
He drew his sword as if he meant to kill Circe.

Circe fell to her knees. "Who are you?" she cried.
"Do not kill me! Stay here in my palace,
and trust me, and learn to love me!"
But Odysseus remembered the warning of Hermes.
He made Circe promise to turn his friends back into men,
and to play no more tricks.
Then her maids bathed Odysseus in warm water,
and clothed him in a fresh tunic and cloak.
They set before him and Circe
fine food on silver plates
and sweet wine in golden goblets.

ODYSSEUS TURNED AWAY.
"I cannot eat nor drink
while my companions are still spell-bound," he said.
Then Circe went to the sties
and drove out the herd of pigs.
She smeared each beast with a magic balm
and as she did this, their bristles fell off,
the pigs' snouts disappeared,
and Odysseus saw his dear companions once more.
He wept for joy. Then Circe said,
"Odysseus, go down to the shore
and drag your ship high on the beach.
Then bring the rest of your ship's company back here
and stay with me for a while."

Odysseus did as Circe had asked.
Then he and all the ship's company
remained in Circe's palace for many months,
feasting and singing, and living in soft delight.

A T THE END OF A YEAR, WHEN THEY WERE LEAVING,
Circe warned Odysseus
of the dangers that still lay ahead.
She told him of the Sirens
whose song lured men to death.
She told him of the horrible monsters,
Scylla and Charybdis, and how to escape from them.

ODYSSEUS SAID GOODBYE TO CIRCE
and he and his companions left her island in the ship.
When they were nearing the island of the Sirens,
Odysseus did as Circe had advised him.
He knew that if his sailors heard the Sirens' song
they would sail towards the island
and every man would be lost.
He softened a ball of wax, and with this
he plugged the ears of every man but himself.
He had told Eurylochus to bind him with ropes to the mast,
and not to loosen the ropes, however much he pleaded.

As the ship came near the island,
the Sirens sang an entrancing song.
The sailors could not hear it,
but Odysseus heard it and was filled with longing
to go nearer, to land on the island
and to taste the pleasures promised in the song.
He pleaded with Eurylochus to untie the ropes,
he ordered and he threatened.
But Eurylochus only tightened his bonds
and would not set him free
until they were beyond the reach of the Sirens' song.

Now the ship came into the narrow channel
that lay between Scylla and Charybdis.
The men could already see the spray and churning water
and hear the roar of the whirlpool, Charybdis,
as she sucked the water down under the rocks on her side.
On the other side they saw Scylla,
a monster with six heads, grinning teeth,
and twelve grasping feet
which she dangled out of her cave,
high on the rocks opposite Charybdis.

"Row as quickly as you can,"
Odysseus cried to the oarsmen.
"Steer straight on, but keep nearer to Scylla,
for if the whirlpool catches us,
we shall all be lost," he said to the helmsman.
So the ship sped on, swift as a bird,
between the two dangers.
But they were not quick enough.
With her cruel feet,
Scylla snatched up six of the sailors
and crammed them into her six long-fanged mouths.
Odysseus and the others wept for pity and fear,
but now the ship was through the channel
and out on the open sea.

S O ODYSSEUS CONTINUED HIS JOURNEY
knowing he must face many more dangers.
For Poseidon, the god of the sea,
had sworn that it should take him
ten years before he could reach rocky Ithaca.